S _____ *wall*
m
M
M leth!

ably

Answer - all over, finished, finito, dead as a dormouse.
Splendid. Right, well, everything seems hunky-dory there, Miles. Keep up the good work.
Cheers, Miles.
Cheers, old love. Roger and out. *(He drinks; resumes sitting)* Oh Jeez... what a ghastly bloody canister of worms...

CRESSIDA ENTERS, carrying shoe box and large potted plant.

CRESSIDA: Oh.
MILES: Ah. *(Stands)*
CRESSIDA: You're home.
MILES: Hello, poppet.
CRESSIDA: Hi.
MILES: Hi.

CRESSIDA: I said you're home.

MILES: Yah. I know.

CRESSIDA: Thought you had a late meeting.

MILES: I did.

CRESSIDA: Oh, right... Good day?

MILES: Gruesome.

CRESSIDA: Really?

MILES: Bit like Dante's Inferno without the funny bits.

CRESSIDA: Oh, what a shame. Can you fix me a little drinkie? *(She goes into kitchen with plant)*

MILES: Mmm... can do. G and T?

CRESSIDA: *(Off)* Please. *(He pours gin and tonic)* Just got in?

MILES: Yah.

CRESSIDA: You have remembered we're going to Lucinda's?

MILES: Mmm, natch. I've put the Discovery out on the driveway already.

CRESSIDA: Excellent.

MILES: All ready for the off.

CRESSIDA: Great. Lucinda's doing a duck.

MILES: Is she, by God? *(CRESSIDA RE-ENTERS)* One G and T.

CRESSIDA: Oh, wow, that's a big one.

MILES: Thought you liked big ones.

CRESSIDA: I do. Super. *(Brief kiss; they sit)* Whew!

MILES: Cheers.

CRESSIDA: Cheers. Mmm... lovely. Needed that.

MILES: Mmm... what was that flower pot?

CRESSIDA: Plumbago. For Lucinda.

MILES: Ah - right.

CRESSIDA: Yah... caneton aux cerises.

MILES: Sorry?

CRESSIDA: Caneton aux cerises. Duck with cherries.

MILES: Oh. Sounds fantastic.

CRESSIDA: Not mad about duck as a rule.

MILES: No.

CRESSIDA: Can be slightly...

MILES: Yes. Slightly.

CRESSIDA: Slightly on the...

MILES: I agree.

CRESSIDA: By the way, is there something wrong with the alarm?

MILES: Is there?

CRESSIDA: Seems to be some kind of red light flashing away.

MILES: Flashing?

CRESSIDA: On and off.

MILES: Ah.

CRESSIDA: That sort of flashing.

MILES: Yes. Actually...

CRESSIDA: Yes?

MILES: Now you mention it...

CRESSIDA: What?

MILES: Don't think it was working when I came in.

CRESSIDA: Wasn't it?

MILES: Don't actually recall any bleeping noises. Don't think I had to switch it off.

CRESSIDA: Aha.

MILES: I'll take a look later.

CRESSIDA: Right. Might have to call the people in.

MILES: Mmm...

CRESSIDA: I mean - bit peeving if it's gone non-op.

MILES: I'll have a look in a mo.

CRESSIDA: Like an olive?

MILES: Not really.

CRESSIDA: Oh. Right. Oh - do you want to see my shoes?

MILES: Shoes?

CRESSIDA: New shoes.

MILES: Ah, you got them.

CRESSIDA: *(Unpacks shoes)* Yah, not the ones I thought. But I got these instead.

MILES: Didn't they have the others?

CRESSIDA: They did actually, yes, but... I liked these. What do you think?

MILES: I thought you wanted green.

CRESSIDA: Yah, but... mmm... perhaps I should have taken the green. I thought blue might be more... you know...

MILES: Mmm... Nice.

CRESSIDA: More sort of...

MILES: Yes.

CRESSIDA: Don't you like them?

MILES: Yes, I do. They're nice.

CRESSIDA: *(Puts them on, stands to look at her feet)* Girl was hopeless.

MILES: Uh-huh?

CRESSIDA: Complete wonk. God knows where they find them. Probably ought to be scrubbing a floor somewhere.

MILES: Really?

CRESSIDA: That sort of voice.

MILES: Ah - floor scrubbing voice.

CRESSIDA: You don't like them, do you?

MILES: Yes I do. I'm very fond of blue.

CRESSIDA: Could always go back and get the green as well.

MILES: Mmm...

CRESSIDA: What was that?

MILES: What?

CRESSIDA: Thought I heard something.

MILES: Don't think so.

CRESSIDA: Upstairs. Sort of bump.

MILES: Bump?

CRESSIDA: Like sort of... bumpity-bump.

MILES: Really?

CRESSIDA: Maybe not. *(She sits, takes shoes off, drops them on floor)*

MILES: How was your day, anyway?

CRESSIDA: Oh God, mega-frantic. Christopoulos was in again, looking at the Patrick Heron.

MILES: Was he, by God?

CRESSIDA: I think he'll buy, but he's being awfully cagey. Trying to get the price down, right? Godfrey has to play it very cool.

MILES: Do you think he'll buy?

CRESSIDA: Don't know. Market's horribly flat at the moment. I think Godfrey's a bit desp actually.

MILES: Oh dear.

CRESSIDA: He hasn't said anything.

MILES: No. What time do we have to be at Lucinda's?

CRESSIDA: Oh... usual sort of time. I think I'll go and have my shower, actually.

MILES: Right.

CRESSIDA: Just finish my drink.

MILES: Mmm...

CRESSIDA: Are you all right?

MILES: What?

CRESSIDA: You seem a bit down in the dumps.

MILES: Bit stressed out, to be honest. Didn't have a very fun day.

CRESSIDA: No?

MILES: No. Frightful boo-boo on the Cheeky Chicken account.

CRESSIDA: Oh dear.

MILES: Now the sods won't approve the new TV script. Creative boys all of a doodah, of course, and Lucrezia Borgia tearing her hair out.

CRESSIDA: Oh lumme... What about Rasputin?

MILES: Nowhere to be seen.

CRESSIDA: Typical.

MILES: Faffing about in Amsterdam with the Fat Lady.

CRESSIDA: Bit tiresome.

MILES: Pain in the what-not, really.

CRESSIDA: Yah... sounds like disasterville. *(She rises)* Do take a dekko at that alarm. *(She leaves)*

MILES: *(Rises, pours another drink)* Cheers, Miles. Cheers. Up yours, me old china. *(He drinks. He looks at himself in the mirror)*

I love you, Miles.

God, I love you too, Miles.

I love your steely blue eyes, Miles, the way you hold me so steadily in your gaze, that carefree way you have of -

CRESSIDA: *(Returns)* Miles -

MILES: What?

CRESSIDA: Why is there a kind of...

MILES: Kind of what?

CRESSIDA: Sort of naked woman upstairs?

MILES: Say that again?

CRESSIDA: Strange woman upstairs - in the bedroom.

MILES: Is there?

CRESSIDA: I mean, what's going on, right?

MILES: Don't know what you're talking about, poppet.

CRESSIDA: There's this naked girl, okay? Upstairs.

MILES: Who?

CRESSIDA: I don't know. I assume she's something to do with you.

MILES: Did you say naked?

CRESSIDA: Yah. Like she hasn't got any clothes on.

MILES: Oh I see.

CRESSIDA: That sort of naked.

MILES: Right.

CRESSIDA: Is she a chum of yours or something?

MILES: Don't think so.

CRESSIDA: Well, I mean... who is she?

MILES: I don't know. Haven't set eyes on her, have I? Only just got in.

CRESSIDA: So how do you know she's not a chum of yours?

MILES: Ah - right. Good question. Er... I don't know that she's a chum of mine.

CRESSIDA: Uh-huh?

MILES: I mean, what's she doing?

CRESSIDA: Not much. Sitting at my dressing table without any clothes on.

MILES: But what did she say?

CRESSIDA: Nothing. She just sort of turned round and stared at me. So I came out again.

MILES: Perhaps she's a mute.

CRESSIDA: Possibly.

MILES: You can have naked mutes, you know.

CRESSIDA: I realise that.

MILES: Or maybe escaped from a loony bin.

CRESSIDA: What!?

MILES: You know - some kind of care in the community stunt. *(DEE COMES IN)* Ah -

DEE: Hello, then.

MILES: Hi.

CRESSIDA: I told you.

MILES: Is this the er...

CRESSIDA: Yes.

MILES: She's not naked.

CRESSIDA: Not now she isn't.

DEE: Yeah, I er... I just borrowed this dressing gown, is that all right? I thought - can't sit around with no clothes on all the time, can I?

MILES: Er, no...

DEE: Not really done.

MILES: Absolutely.

DEE: Not in polite circles, anyway. Nice dressing gown, this. Is it real silk?

CRESSIDA: Listen, who are you?

DEE: Oh, sorry. Dee. Call me Dee.

CRESSIDA:) *(together)* Right.

MILES:)

DEE: What's your names, then?

MILES: Er... I'm Miles. And this is Cressida.

DEE: Right - Cressida and Miles. Got it.

CRESSIDA: But I mean... who are you? Where have you come from?

DEE: Come from?

CRESSIDA: I mean, actually, what are you doing here?

DEE: Oh, we won't be here long.

CRESSIDA: We?

DEE: Only I got to wait for Stu. He'll be back soon.

CRESSIDA: Stu?

DEE: Yeah. Short for Stuart.

CRESSIDA: Ah...

DEE: Nice house this, isn't it? Bigger than you'd think from the outside. Did you do it all up like this?

MILES: We had it done, yes. Didn't literally do it ourselves.

DEE: Really, like, tasteful.

MILES: Yes er... all down to Cressida really.

DEE: Smashing. Like in a magazine almost. Lovely bathroom.

CRESSIDA: Glad you like it.

DEE: Oh yeah, definitely approve. Gorgeous taps. Mmm... I love big hunky taps. And you got some nice pictures too. That square one up on the landing, I like that. Sort of modern art. Can't really see what it's of.

CRESSIDA: Of?

DEE: What it's a picture of.

CRESSIDA: Ah. No. It's a Justin le Sage, actually. Gouache.

DEE: Oh yeah? Is it worth much?

CRESSIDA: Look, do you think some kind of explanation might be on the cards here? I mean, this isn't your house, is it?

DEE: My house? No.

CRESSIDA: It's our house.

DEE: Right. Thought it must be.

CRESSIDA: So I mean, why are you, like... wandering about in it?

DEE: Yeah, well, I haven't got any clothes, see? Not here, I mean. Stu took them away.

MILES: What for?

DEE: Taking them up Fulham. He's going to burn them.

MILES: Goodness. Didn't he like them?

DEE: Oh, it's only old jeans and that. Only they got a bit plastered, see? Needed burning.

MILES: Plastered?

DEE: Sort of dye or something - horrible sticky blue stuff. Intruder dye, yeah? Anyway, I wouldn't mind a drink. What have you got?

CRESSIDA: Christ...

MILES: Drink, yes, er... G and T?

DEE: Come again?

MILES: Gin and tonic?

DEE: Oh, right. Got any Southern Comfort?

MILES: Ah... Southern Comfort. Don't think so. Let's have a dekko. Er... no can do, I'm afraid.

DEE: Something else then. What's that there, that brown stuff? I'll have some of that.

MILES: Madeira?

DEE: Yeah, go on, I'll try a drop of that.

MILES: Right. *(Pours Madeira)*

DEE: Mmm... looks all right. Quite appealing. Mmm...

MILES: You want another one, Cressie?

CRESSIDA: Well, I suppose I may as well, yes. While we er... *(Miles pours gins for himself and Cressida. Dee clears glass)*

DEE: Ooh, good stuff that. Delicious.

MILES: Another?

DEE: Yes please. *(Miles pours again. They all sit)* Drink this one a bit more slow.

CRESSIDA: Right. Perhaps we could disentangle this a little.

DEE: Ooh! Feel nice and relaxed now.

CRESSIDA: Oh, good.

DEE: Had a smashing bath. Really luxurious your bathroom. Loads of hot water, that's what I like.

MILES: Mmm. Tell me -

DEE: I had a good go with your loofah as well.

CRESSIDA: Oh, really?

DEE: Loofahs, yeah - a friend of mine had this video once - sort of erotic video. There were these girls in it doing peculiar things with a loofah - know what I mean? Weird. Loofahs always make me think of that now.

MILES: Dee, er...

DEE: I just did me arms with it though, mainly. And me thighs.

MILES: Yes. Perhaps we could er -

DEE: I need to work on me thighs a bit more often. Stu says thighs are really important for a woman.

MILES: Dee, er -

DEE: I think he's right, tell you the truth. Bit crucial, thighs, when you think about it. Sorry - go on.

MILES: How um... How did you actually get in here?

DEE: Get in? What, in here?

MILES: Yes.

DEE: Oh, no prob. Well, Stu got in through the kitchen window first, right?

MILES: Right.

DEE: Then he just let me in the front. He usually makes me do the clambering bits, but we didn't want to spread the dye around too much. Anyway, they're ever so easy, these modern places.

MILES: What about the alarm?

DEE: Oh yeah, he fixed that first - on the outside. In case it was on, see? He's got all the tools and that.

MILES: But how did he get up there?

DEE: What, up the box? Up his ladder.

MILES: I see.

DEE: Never travels without his ladder in the van.

CRESSIDA: Now we know why the red light's blinking away.

DEE: Oh yeah, I noticed that. Stu'll fix that before we go, though, get it all set up again. He's ever so good with alarms - got a sort of way with them. I'll remind him in case he forgets.

CRESSIDA: Oh, thanks.

DEE: Yeah, he wouldn't leave anything crapped up. Well, wouldn't be fair, would it?

CRESSIDA: Of course not.

DEE: I mean, like, suppose you left somebody's alarm off and then somebody broke in and burgled them. See what I mean?

MILES: Right.

DEE: 'Cause you can't be too careful, really, can you? Not these days. You get a lot of break-

ins around here?

MILES: Quite a few, yes. On the increase actually.

DEE: Yeah, terrible... got many valuables in the place?

MILES: Er... a few things, yes.

DEE: What - jewellery and that?

MILES: Things like that, yes.

DEE: Yeah, and your pictures must be worth a few quid too. You got any peanuts or crisps or anything?

MILES: Crisps, er...

CRESSIDA: No. We haven't.

DEE: Oh.

CRESSIDA: We don't eat things like that.

DEE: Oh. Never mind. Just felt like a nibble.

MILES: I think we have some olives.

DEE: Ugh! Hate olives. Really vile.

MILES: Oh - sorry.

DEE: Not to worry. Saves me spoiling me appetite. Hang on, I think I left me ciggies upstairs. *(She leaves)*

MILES: Mmm... intriguing.

CRESSIDA: Listen, Miles - are you going to do anything?

MILES: Yes, of course, er... you mean... ?

CRESSIDA: Like get that wretched girl out of here.

MILES: Yes, I know. Er... bit tricky really.

CRESSIDA: Why?

MILES: She hasn't got any clothes, you see.

CRESSIDA: So what?

MILES: Well, I mean... she can't just toddle off down the street starkers, can she?

CRESSIDA: Why not?

MILES: Ah. I suppose you could lend her something.

CRESSIDA: Oh yes? Piss off, Miles.

MILES: Well, there you are. And what are we going to tell Stu? When he comes.

CRESSIDA: Tell him what you like. If there is a Stu.

MILES: If there is a Stu? You mean - ?

CRESSIDA: Exactly.

MILES: Touch of the figments perhaps.

CRESSIDA: Right.

MILES: Hadn't thought of that.

CRESSIDA: Or just call the police, for God's sake.

MILES: Could do, yes. Bit of a tricksy situation really.

CRESSIDA: Well, do something, Miles, please. This is really peeving.

MILES: Yes, yes, I will.

DEE RE-ENTERS smoking cigarette.

DEE: All right, then? *(She takes another drink and sits)* Mmm... nice this stuff. Bit of body to it. What's it called again?

MILES: Madeira.

DEE: Madeira, right. I expect Stu's tried it.

MILES: Ah, Stu, yes...

DEE: He's more for knocking back the beer, though. Real ale and that. You got an ashtray?

MILES: Er...

CRESSIDA: We don't smoke.

DEE: Oh, right. Wish I didn't, really. Use this, shall I?

MILES: Oh, er - sure.

DEE: Yeah, keep saying I'll give up but I never seem to.

MILES: Not easy, I imagine.

DEE: No. Stu smokes these roll-ups. Too strong for me.

MILES: Right.

DEE: You can get these nicotine patches now, you know. Stick on your arm and that, help you give up. I might try them.

MILES: Yes, good idea. Er...

DEE: When I said to Stu about the patches he said yeah, only I'd need to stick it over me mouth - cheeky sod.

MILES: Uh-huh. Now the thing is, er, Dee -

DEE: I know I talk too much. I can't help it.

MILES: The thing is.

DEE: What's that?

MILES: Let me put it this way.

DEE: Uh-huh?

MILES: I mean, er -

CRESSIDA: Oh, for God's sake get on with it, Miles!

MILES: Yes, okay, just give me a chance, okay?

CRESSIDA: I mean, for Pete's sake!

MILES: I'm trying to put this diplo... What we don't understand er... Dee...

DEE: Uh-huh?

MILES: Well, for instance, this friend of yours, Stu...

DEE: Stu - yeah?

MILES: What do you and Stu... actually want? I mean, it's a bit off, really, isn't it, to er..?

CRESSIDA: Break into somebody's house?

DEE: Break in?

CRESSIDA: Force your way in.

DEE: There's no sign of a break-in.

CRESSIDA: That's beside the point.

DEE: We haven't broken anything. Stu's ever so careful.

MILES: Yes, of course he is, but...

DEE: If we have, we'll replace it - no prob. But we haven't. Actually, I think Stu'll want to take the loofah away, just to be on the safe side, but we'll get you a new one.

MILES: Fine. Okay. The question is - why are you here?

DEE: Right.

CRESSIDA: Right.

DEE: Yeah, the thing is it's probably best if Stu explains. When he comes.

CRESSIDA: Why can't you explain?

DEE: Well, I can. Only it's a bit sort of complicated. I mean, I'm not saying you wouldn't understand. Like I wouldn't want to insult you or anything but... It's all the ins and outs, you see. All happened in a rush.

CRESSIDA: Try.

DEE: Well, all right, if you like. But don't blame me if it's confusing, right?

CRESSIDA: Right.

DEE: Er... can you get me another drink please, Miles. *(Miles pours her another drink)* Think I'm going to need this. Thanks. Ooh... nice. Mmm... stronger than it looks, this stuff, isn't it? Sort of potent. Anyway, where was I?

CRESSIDA: You were telling us why you're here.

DEE: Oh, yeah. Well, first of all, we needed somewhere for me to go for a bit, somewhere close, right? Where I'm out of sight.

MILES: Right.

DEE: Then afterwards -

CRESSIDA: Just a moment - why did you need somewhere to go?

MILES: Hang on, Cressie -

CRESSIDA: Shut up, Miles.

MILES: No, hang on a mo -

CRESSIDA: Shut up!

MILES: Right.

CRESSIDA: Now then - why did you need somewhere to go?

DEE: Well, I mean, obviously, so's I'm out of sight for a bit.

CRESSIDA: Out of sight of what?

DEE: Well, everybody.

CRESSIDA: What for?

MILES: Till the coast's clear?

DEE: Yeah.

MILES: Obviously.

DEE: Obviously.

CRESSIDA: Why?

DEE: Oh God... So's I could get cleaned up, wait for Stu to get back from Fulham, bring me some new clothes.

CRESSIDA: What for?

DEE: Oh blimey, this is like the third degree. Why, what for, why, why, why! Are you always like this? Is she always like this?

CRESSIDA: *(Rising)* For Christ's sake! Look - this is my house, right?

DEE: Yeah, I know that.

CRESSIDA: And you're just -

DEE: Look -

CRESSIDA: No - you look.

MILES: Hang on, Cressie -

CRESSIDA: And all you can do is blather and bleat like a grade six wimp as usual.

MILES: Cressie, darling, just calm down a fraction, okay?

CRESSIDA: No - why should I?

DEE: I mean, I'm only sitting here. I don't see what all the frigging fuss is about. I'm sorry I borrowed your dressing gown. I'll take it off if you like. Your husband can look at me tits all evening.

CRESSIDA: This is madness. I'm calling the police.

DEE: Yeah, well, you might find that a bit difficult, actually.

CRESSIDA: What do you mean?

DEE: Stu fixed the phone, didn't he?

CRESSIDA: I beg your pardon?

DEE: Just a precaution. Till we go. Then he'll connect you up again. He's brilliant with phones. *(CRESSIDA lifts phone, tries a few buttons, slams it down again)* Told you.

CRESSIDA: Right!

DEE: Right.

CRESSIDA: Okay... let's all sit down again.

DEE: I'm sitting down already.

CRESSIDA: *(Sits)* Now then...

DEE: What now?

CRESSIDA: I'm counting to forty.

Some time elapses.

DEE: Slow counter, isn't she?

CRESSIDA: *(Rising)* Fucking hell!

DEE: Ooh, charming...?

MILES: *(Rising)* Cressie, darling, listen –

DEE: Not very ladylike.

CRESSIDA: Fuck! Fuck! Fuck! *(CRESSIDA LEAVES)*

DEE: Well I never.

MILES: Oh sh... *(He starts to follow her, stands indecisively)* Look er... I'm sorry about that. She's a bit upset.

DEE: Oh yeah? What about?

MILES LEAVES, RETURNS immediately.

MILES: I think perhaps er... just give her a chance to...

DEE: Yeah. Probably best.

MILES: Anyway er... Look, Dee, I think we'd better er...

DEE: What?

MILES: Well, um... how long do you think Stu's going to be?

DEE: *(Rises, moves about)* Stu? Couple of hours. As long as he's not picked up.

MILES: What do you mean?

DEE: Still, they've never managed to get him before. Shouldn't think there's much chance really.

MILES: No. Right.

DEE: Easier for him to get through without me, all covered in blue stuff. That's what I was explaining.

MILES: What?

DEE: Well, obviously, stop the van with me plastered in blue muck - dead giveaway.

MILES: Yes, of course. Well, I suppose we'll just have to wait.

DEE: Yeah.

MILES: Thing is, you see, we're planning to pop out later.

DEE: Uh-huh.

MILES: Visit some friends in Peckham.

DEE: That's nice. What, dinner party, is it?

MILES: Yes, just a little er... Lucinda's doing a duck.

DEE: Is she?

MILES: Caneton something or other. Duck with cherries.

DEE: Mmm... sounds delicious.

MILES: Yes, she er... dab hand with duck. As a rule.

DEE: Uh-huh. Well, don't hang about for me. You just go.

MILES: Right... What blue muck?

DEE: Sort of dye. I don't know. Squirted all over me as soon as I got inside Took ages to scrub off. That's how your loofah got mucked up.

MILES: I see... Got inside what?

DEE: What?

CRESSIDA returns to collect her shoes.

MILES: Cressie - er -

CRESSIDA: I'm having my shower now and getting ready.

MILES: Ah. Excellent notion.

CRESSIDA: Then I'm going to Lucinda's.

MILES: Right.

CRESSIDA: You can do what the fuck you like.

MILES: Cressie, poppet -

CRESSIDA: Just... just drop dead, Miles. Okay?

MILES: Okay. Sure. Right away.

CRESSIDA leaves.

Dearie me.

DEE: No blue stuff on me now, though.

MILES: Oh. Good.

DEE: Clean as a whistle.

MILES: Right.

DEE: Yeah, borrowed some of your wife's body lotion - white musk and mango. Reckon I'm fresh as a daisy now.

MILES: Mmm... I wonder if er...

DEE: *(Yawns)* Ooh... starting to feel sleepy all of a sudden.

MILES: Really?

DEE: Yeah, busy day. Bit knackered now. Feel like curling up in a nice bed. *(Sits)* You know - with somebody nice.

MILES: Ah. Like.... Stu?

DEE: Stu? Yeah, when he don't stink of beer. And chemicals.

MILES: Oh dear.

DEE: I mean, Stu's all right. Plenty of energy and that, but... you see, what I really need...

MILES: What?

DEE: Well, Stu - I mean, bit like getting into bed with a Rottweiler.

MILES: Oh Lord.

DEE: Yeah, know what I mean?

MILES: Er... haven't actually had that experience myself.

DEE: Bet you're not like that. Bet you're the refined sort of type. Eh? In bed, I mean. Artistic sort of lover.

MILES: Me?

DEE: Yeah, I can imagine. Know how to arouse a woman's body. Am I right?

MILES: Oh no, I wouldn't er... Oh dear... Not sure where this conversation's leading us.

DEE: No?

MILES: Did you say chemicals?

DEE: Chemicals?

MILES: Didn't you say chemicals?

DEE: When was that?

Sound of nearby explosion.

Oh Christ! There she goes! *(Rises)*

MILES: What the hell was that?

DEE: Bloody loud too.

MILES: What was it?

DEE: Sounded like an explosion.

MILES: That's what I thought. *(Looks out of the window)* Can't see anything.

DEE: No.

MILES: Wonder what -

DEE: Over Tutley Park way, I think.

MILES: Really?

DEE: That's where it sounded like, didn't it?

MILES: Maybe just a car back-firing.

DEE: Don't think so. Too loud.

MILES: Tutley Park? Isn't that - ?

DEE: What?

MILES: Isn't that the - ?

DEE: MOD Place, yeah.

MILES: MOD - oh Lord! You don't think it could be.... well, terrorists or something?

DEE: Don't know. Could be, I suppose.

MILES: I mean, I don't know what they get up to in there but... all fenced off usually. Big iron railings, barbed wire and so on.

DEE: Telling me.

MILES: *(At window)* Oh I say, look at that - huge cloud of smoke coming up.

DEE: Oh yeah...

MILES: Smokeless zone too - supposed to be.

DEE: Oh dear.

MILES: Won't please the residents association. Probably just something gone off accidentally, though, don't you think? Some sort of balls-up Mother Brown?

DEE: Mmm, probably. What do you make the time?

MILES: Time? Er... ten to seven.

DEE: Yeah, gone off hours too early.

MILES: Really?

DEE: Like activated prematurely. Something wrong with the timer.

MILES: You think so?

DEE: Definitely.

MILES: But what makes you - ?

CRESSIDA ENTERS in dressing gown.

CRESSIDA: Did you hear that zonking great noise?

MILES: Yah. Something gone pop somewhere. Terrorists maybe. Have you seen all the smoke and fumes?

CRESSIDA: No. Oh God, look at it.

MILES: Funny colour too. Sort of pink.

CRESSIDA: Pink?

MILES: Well, flamingo pink or -

CRESSIDA: That's not pink.

MILES: What is it then?

CRESSIDA: More sort of... oh well, you never did have much colour sense, Miles.

MILES: Yes I did. Do.

CRESSIDA: No you don't.

MILES: What would you call it then - peach?

CRESSIDA: Peach? For pity's sake...

DEE: I'd call it pink.

CRESSIDA: Oh. You're still here.

DEE: Yeah, afraid so. Can't go yet, can I? Till Stu gets here.

MILES: We're still waiting for Stu.

CRESSIDA: Are we?

MILES: Apparently.

DEE: Only thing is er... he might be a bit delayed now, you see.

CRESSIDA: Delayed?

DEE: Because of the explosion.

CRESSIDA: Why?

Sounds of fire engines and police cars.

MILES: There they go. Jolly quick too - full marks.

DEE: Well, obviously er... roads all gunged up with fire engines and that...

MILES: Bound to play havoc with the traffic.

CRESSIDA: Mmm... how convenient.

DEE: Depends though. I mean, if he's on his way back already he might just push on regardless. Difficult to tell with Stu - bit unpredictable.

CRESSIDA: Is he?

DEE: Wouldn't want me stranded here in the middle of it, anyway. Much too risky.

CRESSIDA: What do you mean?

MILES: It's coming closer - sort of wafting this way.

CRESSIDA: Oh God, so it is. You don't suppose it could be poisonous, do you?

DEE: Ah, yeah... could be.

MILES: Dee thinks it's over in Tutley Park - MOD place.

CRESSIDA: Really?

DEE: Yeah, chemical warfare research. They got all sorts in there, Stu says. Probably a load of way out stuff gone up in smoke.

MILES: Looks to me like the whole caboodle's gone west.

CRESSIDA: Oh no! Isn't that utterly typical? I mean, what do they think they're playing at, having a set-up like that in a residential neighbourhood?

MILES: Well, there you are. Mind you, they've got to do it somewhere.

CRESSIDA: Have they?

MILES: I assume so.

CRESSIDA: Why can't they do it on Salisbury Plain?

MILES: No idea. Probably something to do with grazing rights.

CRESSIDA: Surely that's big enough for them.

MILES: Ah, but size isn't everything.

CRESSIDA: So you keep telling me.

More fire engine sounds.

MILES: Gosh - they're certainly out in force. Tally-ho!

CRESSIDA: Well, I think it's abominably peeving. I mean, who wants another Chernobyl on the doorstep? I shall make my father write to somebody about this.

MILES: Who?

CRESSIDA: I don't know, do I? But I mean, if that awful yucky smoke blows in on us it could affect my shrubs or even discolour the patio or something. It looks really invasive.

MILES: Invasive - that's a good word. Like invasive surgery.

CRESSIDA: And you're not doing a damned thing about it.

MILES: No. Sorry.

CRESSIDA: Just drooping about like a broken reed.

MILES: Yes, but... I don't know what you imagine I can do. Anyway, broken reeds don't droop.

CRESSIDA: Don't they? What do they do?

MILES: Just lie down, I think.

CRESSIDA: Yes, that sounds like you. Meanwhile, we're no closer to solving our other little problem, are we?

MILES: Aren't we? What's that?

CRESSIDA: Oh God, Miles, I do have doubts sometimes about your attention span. Her!

MILES: Ah - yes.

CRESSIDA: Because unless this alleged Stu character turns up, we can't even go to Lucinda's, can we? At least, you can't.

MILES: No.

CRESSIDA: I can.

MILES: Yes.

CRESSIDA: And I will.

MILES: Right.

CRESSIDA: I mean it, Miles.

MILES: I believe you.

CRESSIDA: This explosion changes nothing.

MILES: Of course not.

CRESSIDA: Just in case you think it does.

MILES: Absolutely.

CRESSIDA: I mean it, Miles.

MILES: You've said that already.

CRESSIDA: Have I?

MILES: Pretty certain.

DEE: Er... excuse me.

CRESSIDA: What?

DEE: Just thought - might be an idea to check you got all your windows closed and that. Block your front door a bit. Make sure the smoke can't come in, right?

CRESSIDA: Yes - probably.

MILES: Actually it seems to be thinning out a fraction. May not even reach us.

DEE: Yeah but... just to be on the safe side.

MILES: Yes. Good thinking, Dee.

CRESSIDA: All right. I'll do that.

MILES: Okay.

CRESSIDA: Then I'm having my shower.

MILES: Super idea.

CRESSIDA: Then I'm going to Lucinda's.

MILES: Sure.

CRESSIDA: You can just... drop dead, Miles. Okay?

MILES: Ah. Haven't we had this conversation already? *(CRESSIDA leaves)* Oh God... cannon to left of them, cannon to right of them volleyed and thundered.

DEE: Do what?

MILES: Into the jaws of death rode the six hundred.

DEE: Oh, right... Smoke's definitely clearing, by the way.

MILES: Is it? *(Sits with head in hands)*

DEE: Think so. Sort of subsiding.

MILES: Fine.

DEE: Shall we have another drink?

MILES: If you like.

DEE: Yeah, why not?

MILES: Their's not to make reply, their's not to reason why...

DEE: *(Pours drinks, sits, lights cigarette)* Here we go, then.

MILES: Thanks a million.

DEE: You're welcome.

MILES: Awfully peculiar day this. Odd. Sort of dream-like.

DEE: Uh-huh?

MILES: As if I'd slipped through a crack in the system, into some alternative universe or black hole or something. I felt so positive this morning. Sun shining, Cressie all sweetness and light, footsie up forty-five points following interest rate hopes on Wall Street. I was rather looking forward to the Cheeky Chicken meeting, and when Lucrezia Borgia decided to sit in on it I thought - big chance to shine here, Miles, show her what you're made of, show her there's a pair of balls tucked away down there inside the boxers. Oh yes, it was all fire-in-the-belly, get-up-and-

go-for-it-kid. Started off okay on all the introductory bullshit - everything fine and dandy. Then I happened to glance in Lucrezia's direction and I... I suddenly realised that she was the spitting image of a python. You know - mean little eyes, tongue forking in and out and all that, bags of venom in reserve. Suddenly felt rather queasy. Then I heard myself stammering. Then the client interrupted me. Then he dropped his bombshell. Steady, Miles. Steady, old boy. Remember the drill. What baffles me is this - why have I always been in a state of subjugation to some tyrannical woman? Mmm? Don't understand it. Can't fathom it out. Mother was the worst - last of the big potty trainers. Actually she wasn't the worst - take that back - sorry, Mummy. Rosemary Rutter was the worst - foul woman who ran the Conservatives at Oxford. Spent nearly three years as her dogsbody. Then came Sally, the Sittingbourne sadist. Then came Cressie. Actually Cressie's not so bad even if she does treat me like a third world baggage handler. Then came Lucrezia.

Sound of police cars.

Day to day, minute to minute, I've always had the feeling that I was making decisions, making choices, even if it was just kidology. But today I can't even work up the illusion of being in control. I feel I'm just being blown around in a different universe - one that looks quite like this one, it's true, but... not the same. Just billowing about in it like all that pink smoke. *(He rises, goes to the mirror)*

Hello, Miles.

Hello, old boy - still in the land of the living then?

Yep - still hanging on. Skin of the teeth and all that.

That's the spirit, Miles.

Absolutely.

One thing I want you to know, Miles.

What's that, old love?

If anything should... well, if anything should happen to you, Miles....

Yes?

I want you to know - I will wait for you.

No!

Yes! I don't care what you've done, Miles. I don't care what the others say. I'm in love with you, dammit. And no matter what happens... however long it takes... I'll be here... I'll be waiting for you.

DEE rises, stands behind Miles and looks in the mirror.

Oh, Miles, I don't know what to say.

He gazed back at him. His clear blue eyes spoke of compassion, of faithfulness, of a love beyond words...

DEE: Nice-looking, your friend.

MILES: Yes.

DEE: Look at me instead. *(MILES turns to face her)* Do you like me?

MILES: Yes.

DEE: Yeah, thought you might. *(They kiss)* There you are.

MILES: Yes.

DEE: Nice?

MILES: Yes.

DEE: Do it again?

STU ENTERS from kitchen with bundle of clothes.

STU: Right. That's that sorted.

MILES: Oh my God - sorry.

DEE: Ah - at last.

STU: All right?

DEE: Yeah.

STU: All right, mate?

MILES: Er... think so, yes.

DEE: You took your time.

STU: Yeah. Traffic.

DEE: Told you.

STU: Getting back was a real sod. Nose to tail through Wandsworth. All right, though. Didn't get stopped.

DEE: Just as well. You know it's bleeding well gone off already?

STU: Yeah, course I do, stupid. Heard it, didn't I? Couldn't miss that.

DEE: Timer must have got screwed up.

STU: Telling me. I'll nail that fucking Titch to the wall when I see him. You all cleaned up?

DEE: Oh, yeah. I'm fine.

STU: Right. Fingernails?

DEE: Yeah, yeah. What about my stuff?

STU: Yeah, all seen to. Burnt to a cinder.

DEE: Great. This is Miles, by the way.

STU: Oh yeah?

MILES: Yes er... hi there. You must be Stu.

DEE: Stu, yeah.

STU: Got a beer, mate?

MILES: What?

STU: Beer - you got a beer?

MILES: Er... might just have a lager in the fridge.

STU: That'll do.

MILES: Right, I'll just er... shan't be a mo. *(Goes into the kitchen)*

DEE: Is that me clean gear?

STU: Yeah. *(Hands over the clothing)*

DEE: Where's me underwear?

STU: Didn't bother with that.

DEE: Oh Christ...

STU: You got all that dye off? That's the main thing.

DEE: Yeah, I told you. I'm fine.

STU: Okay.

DEE: Yeah er... I mucked up one or two things here, though. Couple of towels and that. And a loofah.

STU: That's all right. Don't worry about that.

DEE: Shall we bring them with us?

STU: Bring them with us? You thick or what?

DEE: But I thought -

STU: Well, don't think. I'll do that.

DEE: Right. So what we doing? We going now?

STU: Yeah. Er...

DEE: What?

STU: Got another problem.

DEE: What's that?

STU: Dye all over the inside of the van.

DEE: Oh shit!

STU: Yeah... on the back of the seat. All soaked in. Told you not to touch the seat.

DEE: I didn't. I stayed on the tarpaulin.

STU: Yeah, well, you must have done. And on the front tyre.

DEE: Oh, bugger it!

STU: Thing is, they'll have road blocks all over the place by now.

DEE: So what we going to do? Stay here?

STU: No. No future in that. Want to get up north tonight.

DEE: What, then?

MILES ENTERS with can and glass.

MILES: Right. Here we are, guv'nor. One lager.

STU: Cheers, mate. *(Drinks from can)* Ah! That's better.

MILES: Jolly good. Thirsty work er...

STU: What is?

MILES: Driving around er... I mean across London... I should imagine.

STU: Yeah... Dee been keeping you entertained, has she?

MILES: Yes, she er... we had quite a chat really.

STU: Yeah, so I saw. She's good at that.

Sound of police cars.

Right. Better get rolling.

DEE: What about the van - all the blue stuff?

STU: That's all right. I got a plan for that. *(Finishes lager, hands can back to Miles)* Cheers, mate.

MILES: Cheers.

STU: Nice place you got here.

MILES: Yes it's er... not bad.

STU: Nice neighbours?

MILES: Oh... yes. Don't see too much of them, of course. Very quiet neighbourhood really.

STU: Yeah.

MILES: Not a lot happening.

STU: No.

MILES: Not as a rule.

STU: *(To Dee)* Come on, then.

DEE: Hang on - I got to get me clothes on.

STU: Do it on the way. Come on - shift your arse. *(STU LEAVES)*

DEE: Oh blimey... look, I'll have to borrow your wife's dressing gown for a bit, is that all right?

MILES: Oh. Er...

DEE: I'll have it dry cleaned and send it back, yeah?

MILES: Right. I suppose so, yes.

DEE: Only he gets ever so impatient sometimes. Bit of a short fuse.

MILES: Of course.

DEE: Thanks ever so much. See you then.

MILES: See you.

She goes to Miles, gives him a quick kiss.

DEE: Bye. *(Leaves)*

MILES: Bye.

Mmm... ships that pass in the night. Intriguing.

Short fuse?

He goes to the mirror.

Hi there, Miles.

Hi.

I think we may be pulling through, old love.

I think we may, Miles.

One more of life's hurdles behind us, eh? Another little knotty one given the old heave-ho?

Absolutely, skipper.

Blue skies ahead, Miles?

Crest of the wave, sir.

Something to celebrate - what do you think?

Took the words out of my mouth, old boy.

G and T?

Just what the doctor ordered.

He goes to drinks, pours a gin and tonic.

Cheers, Miles. Cheers. Up yours, me old china. *(He drinks)* Okay, Miss Lucrezia so-called-

bloody-Borgia, let's get this out in the open, shall we? Let's stop beating about the bushy-tails for once. I mean, let's get to the bottom line, right? Okay, so there's been a bit of a bloody awful blip - granted et cetera, sackcloth and ashes, humble pie-R-squared and so forth. But look at it from this angle, sweetie - there's a fantastic window of opportunity opening up here for the agency, provided - provided - we've got the balls to get up off our fannies, get out there on the park, pick up the ball -

CRESSIDA ENTERS with loofah and towels.

CRESSIDA: Look at this, Miles!

MILES: Oh Lord - what a mess.

CRESSIDA: Have you ever seen anything like it?

MILES: No. It's that blue dye stuff.

CRESSIDA: The loofah's a total write-off.

MILES: So I see.

CRESSIDA: And the towels are all sort of... impregnated with it. Really gross. *(She throws them down)* Ugh! Horrid. And there's a big nasty splodge on the bathroom carpet.

MILES: Oh dear. Did you have a nice shower, though? That's the main thing.

CRESSIDA: All right, I suppose. Where is she, anyway?

MILES: Ah - gone.

CRESSIDA: Gone?

MILES: Vamoosed. Stu came and picked her up.

CRESSIDA: Oh.

MILES: That sort of gone.

CRESSIDA: He's real, then?

MILES: Yes, I think so. Looked pretty real. Downed a lager, then they skedaddled.

CRESSIDA: I see. Well... count your blessings.

MILES: One by one - yah.

CRESSIDA: What was he like?

MILES: Stu? Bit of a trog really. You know - normal sort of yobbo.

CRESSIDA: Surprise, surprise.

MILES: Only thing is...

Sound of police cars.

CRESSIDA: What?

MILES: Dee had to er... borrow your dressing gown.

CRESSIDA: You're joking.

MILES: No, I'm not. I'm sorry but... nothing I could do really, in the circumstances.

CRESSIDA: What circumstances?

MILES: Stu was in rather a hurry when it came to the point.

CRESSIDA: What point?

MILES: Point of departure. Seemed anxious about the traffic.

CRESSIDA: Uh-huh... well, one dressing gown down the Swanee.

MILES: I fear so, yes. Far, far away.

CRESSIDA: Only my old one, I suppose.

MILES: Oh, jolly good.

CRESSIDA: Just about ready for famine relief. By the way, has all that ghastly smoke cleared?

MILES: Ah - haven't looked recently. Better take a dekko. *(Goes to the window)* More or less evaporated. Just a bit of haze left.

CRESSIDA: That's a relief. Still an awful lot of police cars and things whizzing around though.

MILES: *(Still at window)* Yes. I say, that's funny.

CRESSIDA: What's that?

MILES: Car parked opposite with two chaps sitting in it.

CRESSIDA: So?

MILES: They look a bit fishy.

CRESSIDA goes to the window.

One of them's talking on a mobile.

CRESSIDA: Oh yes. Looking this way now.

MILES: Probably casing the joint.

CRESSIDA: Are you serious?

MILES: No. They wouldn't make it so obvious.

CRESSIDA: I suppose not. Ugly pair of brutes, all the same.

MILES: Hello - driving off.

CRESSIDA: Yes.

MILES: Probably just lost their way somewhere.

CRESSIDA: Mmm... probably. *(They move away from the window)* Right. Well, that's that, is it?

MILES: I guess so, yes. Just let the dust settle.

CRESSIDA: Dust?

MILES: Metaphorically speaking.

CRESSIDA: Oh God -

MILES: What?

CRESSIDA: Did he fix the phone?

MILES: Who? Oh, Stu. Damn - forgot about that.

CRESSIDA: Oh, honestly!

MILES: Sorry, poppet. Slipped my mind.

CRESSIDA: *(Goes to phone, lifts handset)* Seems to be working, though.

MILES: Is it?

CRESSIDA: *(Presses some buttons)* It's ringing. Hello? No, it's okay - wrong number. What? Oh, piddle off, you stupid old pervert. *(Replaces phone)* Yah - all systems go.

MILES: Super-duper.

CRESSIDA: How peculiar.

MILES: Perhaps he did it when I wasn't looking. Or on the outside.

CRESSIDA: What about the alarm, I wonder? *(LEAVES)*

MILES: Alarm? Oh yes - bit crucial.

CRESSIDA: *(Re-entering)* Light's not flashing any more.

MILES: No?

CRESSIDA: Just the little green one to show it's all ready steady go.

MILES: He must have fixed it. Isn't that sporting of him?

CRESSIDA: Very.

MILES: Jolly decent, I think. Just shows - shouldn't judge a chap by his cover.

CRESSIDA: Anyway, we'd better go. We're horrendously late already.

MILES: Go?

CRESSIDA: Lucinda's. You haven't forgotten again? *(Goes into the kitchen)*

MILES: No, of course not.

CRESSIDA: *(Off)* I mean, we can't let her down.

MILES: No.

CRESSIDA: *(Returns from kitchen with potted plant)* Especially if she spent all afternoon cooped up with that duck.

MILES: Yes, indeed.

CRESSIDA: You'll just have to come as you are, I suppose. You don't look too dismal. Prop the plumbago up in the wagon somewhere, would you?

MILES: Sure.

CRESSIDA: Be with you in a mo. Just do something about... *(MILES LEAVES with the potted plant. CRESSIDA picks up towels and loofah)* Oh God, honestly... a plague of boils on the woman. *(Throws them on the floor again. MILES returns with plant)*

MILES: Discovery seems to have gone.

CRESSIDA: Gone?

MILES: Doesn't appear to be there. Sort of vanished into thin air.

CRESSIDA: What are you talking about?

MILES: The Discovery - the car - not there any more.

CRESSIDA: You mean someone's taken it?

MILES: Well... assume so.

CRESSIDA: Didn't you alarm it?

MILES: Yes, of course I did.

CRESSIDA: Then how could - ? Oh no...

MILES: Thing is -

CRESSIDA: What?

MILES: There's a big sort of battered grey van standing there instead. On the driveway.

CRESSIDA: Grey van? Oh my God...

MILES: Well, a sort of dark bluish grey.

CRESSIDA: I don't think the colour matters awfully.

MILES: No. Do you want to go and look?

(CRESSIDA LEAVES)

Steady, Miles. Steady old boy. Worse things happen at sea.

I know they do, Miles.

Spot of crisis management needed here. Choppy water ahead, so keep your eye on the button.

Right, skipper.

Finger on the ball, nose to the tiller - all that.

(CRESSIDA RETURNS)

What do you think?

CRESSIDA: You're right.

MILES: Thought so.

CRESSIDA: Spot on for once.

MILES: Oh dear.

CRESSIDA: Yes.

Sound of police cars.

MILES: Shit!

CRESSIDA: Exactly.

MILES: Shit, shit, shit!

CRESSIDA: All your fault.

MILES: No it wasn't.

CRESSIDA: Yes it was.

MILES: That's not fair.

CRESSIDA: You let them in.

MILES: I did not.

More police cars. Flashing blue lights visible through window. Sounds of police radios.

Gosh - the fuzz are right outside now.

CRESSIDA: Making an abysmal din too.

MILES: Still looking for the terrorists, I expect.

CRESSIDA: Terrorists? Oh - the explosion.

MILES: Exactly. Won't want to be bothered about missing cars.

CRESSIDA: No, I suppose not. Well, we'll just have to report it later. I'd better give Lucinda a ring and then see if I can rustle up a taxi. God, what a perfectly vexing day. *(Goes to phone)*

MILES: Difficult to get a taxi, I should think, with all this commotion raging away.

CRESSIDA: I know that, but I'm not letting Lucinda down. Oh no...

MILES: What?

CRESSIDA: Line's gone dead again.

MILES: No!

CRESSIDA: Isn't that utterly typical? *(She slams down the phone)*

MILES: Why do you think that is?

CRESSIDA: How the hell should I know? Bloody Telecom again.

Sudden sound of hammering at front door.

God almighty! Who's that now?

MILES: Don't know. Oh - could be the fuzz, couldn't it?

CRESSIDA: Fuzz?

MILES: Probably doing a housey-housey. I mean house-to-house.

CRESSIDA: Really?

MILES: You know, because of the fireworks. Routine enquiry. Looking for anything suspicious.

CRESSIDA: Ah - yes.

MILES: Suspicious substances or...

Renewed hammering at front door.

... anything incriminating.

CRESSIDA: Yes.

MILES: Oh Lord... Cressie?

CRESSIDA: What?

MILES: Are you thinking what I'm thinking?

CRESSIDA: I don't know. What are you thinking?

MILES: Buggered if I know.

CRESSIDA: Nor do I.

More hammering.

MILES: Mmm... Well.... better answer it I suppose before they...

CRESSIDA: Yes.

MILES: ... break the door down or...

CRESSIDA: Yes.

MILES: ... something silly like that.

CRESSIDA: Yes.

MILES: I mean, one does hear about these nightmare situations where...

More hammering.

Steady, Miles. Steady, old boy.

Sounds of front door being broken in, shouting etc. MILES and CRESSIDA stand rigid.